PHILADELPHIA PHILLIES
ALL-TIME GREATS

BY TED COLEMAN

Book design by Jake Slavik
Cover design by Jake Slavik

Photographs ©: Rob Carr/AP Images, cover (top), 1 (top); Al Messerschmidt/MESSA/AP Images, cover (bottom), 1 (bottom); Library of Congress, 4; Rooney/AP Images, 7; David Durochik/DUROD/AP Images, 9; AP Images, 10; Ron Frehm/AP Images, 12; Tony Tomsic/TOMST/AP Images, 14; Chris Gardner/AP Images, 16; Matt Slocum/AP Images, 19; Larry Radloff/Icon Sportswire, 21

Press Box Books, an imprint of Press Room Editions.

ISBN
978-1-63494-507-3 (library bound)
978-1-63494-533-2 (paperback)
978-1-63494-583-7 (epub)
978-1-63494-559-2 (hosted ebook)

Library of Congress Control Number: 2022901742

Distributed by North Star Editions, Inc.
2297 Waters Drive
Mendota Heights, MN 55120
www.northstareditions.com

Printed in the United States of America
082022

ABOUT THE AUTHOR

Ted Coleman is a freelance sportswriter and children's book author who lives in Louisville, Kentucky, with his trusty Affenpinscher, Chloe.

TABLE OF CONTENTS

ALEXANDER

CHAPTER 1
THE WHIZ KIDS

The Philadelphia Phillies are one of the oldest teams in Major League Baseball (MLB). They started in 1883. Back then, they were called the Philadelphia Quakers. By the 1890s, the team was officially known as the Phillies. They also had one of their first stars in **Ed Delahanty**. He was one of baseball's first power hitters. In 1896, Delahanty hit four home runs in one game.

Even with stars like Delahanty, the Phillies had never finished in first place. That changed in 1915. Led by pitcher **Pete Alexander**, the 1915 team reached the World Series. Alexander was a master of control. He won 31 or more games each season from 1915 to 1917.

However, the Phillies ended up losing the 1915 World Series. After that, they sank back to the bottom for many years. But they did boast another star in outfielder **Chuck Klein**. Few players loved the game as much as Klein. He led the National League (NL) in home runs four times while playing for the Phillies.

In 1950, the Phillies finally became contenders again. Reporters called their young team "the Whiz Kids." Pitcher **Robin Roberts** was only 23 years old in 1950. But he won 20 games for the Phillies. He went on to

CAREER SHUTOUTS
PHILLIES TEAM RECORD
Pete Alexander: 61

ROBERTS
36

7

win 20 or more games in each of the next five seasons. Another 23-year-old was outfielder **Richie Ashburn**. His speed earned him the name "the Tilden Flash." Ashburn spent 12 years with the team.

The Whiz Kids lost the 1950 World Series. After that, it took 30 years for the Phillies to get back to the Fall Classic. In the meantime, they had stars like pitcher **Jim Bunning**. He threw a perfect game for the Phillies in 1964. Outfielder **Dick Allen** won the NL Rookie of the Year Award in 1964. Phillies fans

COLLAPSE

The Phillies had many painful years in their first century. But 1964 was one of the worst. The team coasted in first place nearly the entire season. With 12 games left, the Phillies led the NL by six and a half games. But then they lost 10 games in a row. The St. Louis Cardinals ended up winning the NL.

immediately loved the Pennsylvania native.

Pitchers feared him. Allen hit 204 of his 351

career home runs in Philadelphia.

LUZINSKI
19

CHAPTER 2
FINALLY CHAMPIONS

When the first World Series took place in 1903, MLB had only 16 teams. By 1980, all but one of those teams had won at least one championship. The Phillies were the only team that hadn't. But Philadelphia's time to celebrate finally arrived in 1980. The Phillies reached the World Series and beat the Kansas City Royals in six games.

Manager Dallas Green could count on **Greg Luzinski**. The hulking left fielder was known as "the Bull." The slugger belted 223 home runs in 11 years with the Phillies.

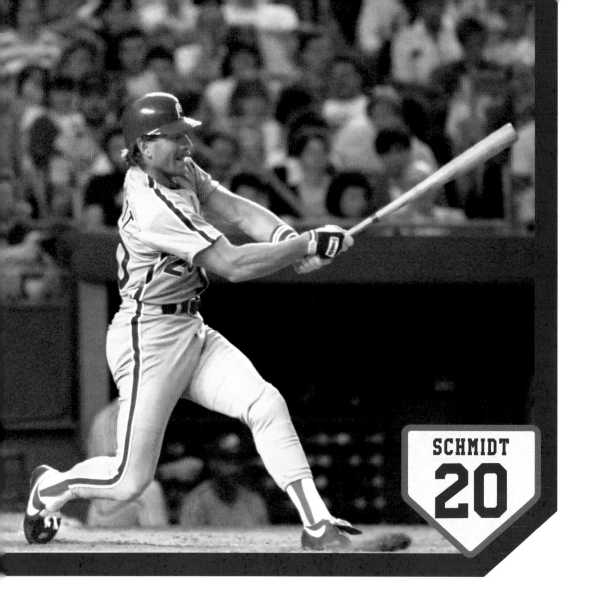

SCHMIDT
20

Superstar third baseman **Mike Schmidt**
led the way. Most Phillies fans consider him
the greatest player in team history. Schmidt
won the first of his three NL Most Valuable

Player (MVP) Awards in 1980. That year, he hit 48 home runs and had 121 runs batted in (RBI). Schmidt was also named MVP of the World Series.

Center fielder **Garry Maddox** brought the speed. His excellent defense held down the outfield. Maddox won the NL Gold Glove Award every year from 1975 to 1982.

Shortstop **Larry Bowa** was never known for his bat. But he stepped up during the 1980 World Series. Bowa batted .375 for the series. He later became the Phillies' manager.

First baseman **Pete Rose** joined the Phillies in 1979. Rose is MLB's all-time leader

STAT SPOTLIGHT

CAREER HOME RUNS
PHILLIES TEAM RECORD
Mike Schmidt: 548

CARLTON
32

in hits. He spent most of his career with the
Cincinnati Reds. But he made a key play for the
Phillies in the 1980 World Series. In the ninth
inning of Game 6, a foul ball was coming down
near the first-base dugout. Philadelphia catcher
Bob Boone dropped it. But Rose snatched
the ball before it hit the turf. One out later, the
Phillies were champions.

The 1980 Phillies also featured one of baseball's best all-time pitchers. Left-hander **Steve Carlton** was a master of the slider. His 4,136 career strikeouts rank fourth in MLB history. He recorded more than 3,000 of those strikeouts with the Phillies. Carlton also won four Cy Young Awards in his career.

Reliever **Tug McGraw** appeared in four of the six World Series games. He had one win and two saves. His second save came in Game 6. McGraw struck out Kansas City's Willie Wilson for the final out.

HARRY KALAS

For nearly 40 years, the Phillies had one of the most beloved radio announcers in baseball. **Harry Kalas** joined the team as a play-by-play man in 1971. Kalas famously loved the song "High Hopes" by Frank Sinatra. At the first game after Kalas's death in 2009, Phillies fans honored him. Fans usually sing "Take Me Out to the Ballgame" during the seventh-inning stretch. But that game, they sang "High Hopes" instead.

DAULTON
10

CHAPTER 3
THE FIGHTIN' PHILS

The Phillies returned to the World Series in 1983 but lost to the Baltimore Orioles. Late that season, **Darren Daulton** had made his debut. It took him six more years to become the starting catcher. But he eventually made three All-Star teams.

Daulton had one of his best seasons in 1993. That year, he hit 24 home runs and had 105 RBIs. He also caught for a very talented pitching staff. **Curt Schilling** had joined the team in 1992. He instantly became the team's ace. His pitching helped Philadelphia reach the World Series the next year. By the 1990s, starting pitchers didn't last as long in games. But Schilling was different. He completed 61 games with the Phillies.

The Phillies lost the 1993 World Series. Then they went on another long playoff drought. But faithful Phillies supporters still came out to see **Bobby Abreu**. The Venezuelan outfielder had a graceful swing. In 2002, he led the NL with 50 doubles.

Shortstop **Jimmy Rollins** joined the Phillies in 2000. Rollins was a classic all-around player. He won four Gold Gloves. But his

LONGEST HITTING STREAK
PHILLIES TEAM RECORD

Jimmy Rollins: 38 games (2005–06)

ROLLINS
11

blazing speed set him apart. He hustled his way to 20 triples in 2007. That led the NL and helped Rollins win the MVP Award.

Everything came together for the Phillies in 2008. They defeated the Tampa Bay Rays for their second World Series title. Slugging first baseman **Ryan Howard** led the way. Second baseman **Chase Utley** also swung for the fences that year. The six-time All-Star blasted a career-high 33 home runs in 2008.

Left-hander **Cole Hamels** anchored the Philadelphia pitching

THE PHILLIE PHANATIC

Every team has a mascot. But only the Phillies have the Phanatic. The large, green mascot is known for his wild antics during games. He often drives around the field on a four-wheeler. Then he shoots hot dogs into the stands. He also heckles opposing players and managers. Some don't like it. Legendary Los Angeles Dodgers manager Tommy Lasorda once attacked the Phanatic when he was taunting the Dodgers dugout.

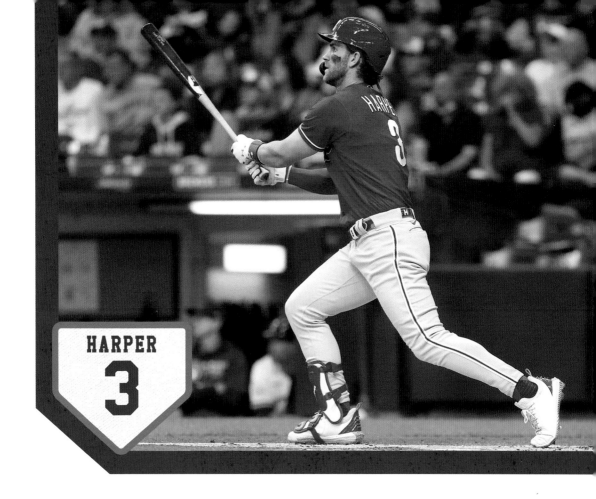

HARPER
3

staff. Hamels threw off batters with his devastating changeup.

In 2019, the Phillies signed another superstar. Fans hoped **Bryce Harper** could lead the team to another World Series title. The Fightin' Phils would no longer accept their history of losing teams.

TIMELINE

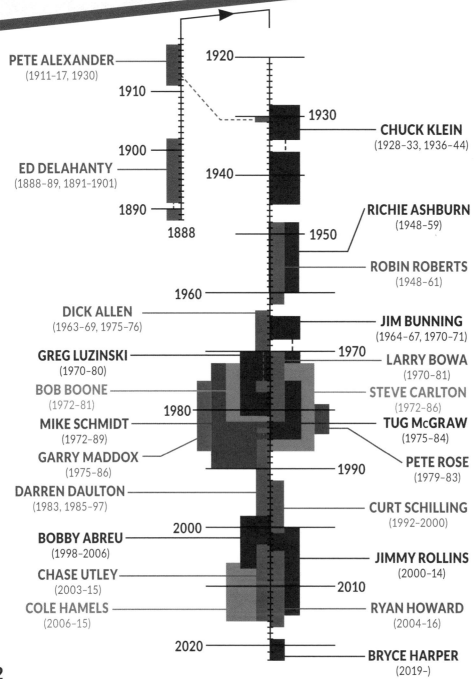

PETE ALEXANDER —
(1911-17, 1930)

1920

1910

CHUCK KLEIN
(1928-33, 1936-44)

1930

1900

ED DELAHANTY —
(1888-89, 1891-1901)

1940

1890

1888

RICHIE ASHBURN
(1948-59)

1950

ROBIN ROBERTS
(1948-61)

1960

DICK ALLEN —
(1963-69, 1975-76)

JIM BUNNING
(1964-67, 1970-71)

GREG LUZINSKI —
(1970-80)

1970

LARRY BOWA
(1970-81)

BOB BOONE —
(1972-81)

STEVE CARLTON
(1972-86)

1980

MIKE SCHMIDT —
(1972-89)

TUG McGRAW
(1975-84)

GARRY MADDOX —
(1975-86)

PETE ROSE
(1979-83)

1990

DARREN DAULTON —
(1983, 1985-97)

CURT SCHILLING
(1992-2000)

2000

BOBBY ABREU —
(1998-2006)

JIMMY ROLLINS
(2000-14)

CHASE UTLEY —
(2003-15)

2010

COLE HAMELS —
(2006-15)

RYAN HOWARD
(2004-16)

2020

BRYCE HARPER
(2019-)

TEAM FACTS

PHILADELPHIA PHILLIES

Team history: Philadelphia Quakers (1883-89), Philadelphia Phillies (1890-)

World Series titles: 2 (1980, 2008)*

Key managers:

Danny Ozark (1973-79)

594-510-1 (.538)

Dallas Green (1979-81)

169-130 (.565), 1 World Series title

Charlie Manuel (2005-13)

780-636 (.551), 1 World Series title

MORE INFORMATION

To learn more about the Philadelphia Phillies, go to **pressboxbooks.com/AllAccess**.

These links are routinely monitored and updated to provide the most current information available.

*through 2021

GLOSSARY

ace
The best starting pitcher on a team.

changeup
A slow pitch that is meant to fool the batter into swinging too early.

contender
A team that is good enough to win a title.

Gold Glove
An award that recognizes the top fielder in the league at each position.

perfect game
A game in which a pitcher doesn't allow any batters to reach base.

reliever
A pitcher who does not start the game.

runs batted in
A statistic that tracks the number of runs that score as the result of a batter's action.

slider
A pitch that moves down and away from the batter.

INDEX